THE MAGIC
OF
GREEN BUCKWHEAT

Nature's Aid to Blood Pressure
and Circulatory Problems

GW00496542

THE MAGIC
OF
GREEN BUCKWHEAT

Nature's Aid to Blood Pressure and Circulatory Problems

by

KATE SPENCER

First edition 1987
Reprinted 1992

© ROMANY HERB PRODUCTS LIMITED 1987
Cover photography by Richard Crease

*All rights reserved. No part of this book may be reproduced or utilized
in any form or by any means, electronic or mechanical, including
photocopying, recording or by any information storage and retrieval
system, without permission in writing from the Publisher.*

ISBN 0 7225 2174 X

Printed and bound in Great Britain by
HarperCollinsManufacturing, Glasgow

Contents

Introduction

Yet again, we have Nature to thank for a kind and gentle plant medicine alternative to drug treatment for a number of ailments particularly prevalent in today's rushed and stressful world.

This time green buckwheat tea, or tablets made from compressed buckwheat leaf and flowers, provide the commercial source of a flavonoid called rutin which has been known for some time to have a beneficial effect on blood vessels, thereby easing a number of associated problems.

Rutin can be especially valuable to sufferers from high blood pressure for it helps to strengthen and increase the efficiency of the small blood vessels — and if blood pressure is high, the pipes which carry the blood must be strong and elastic to cope.

Although rutin occurs in many forms of plant life, buckwheat combines a particularly high rutin and mineral content and thrives especially well in the lush green fields of Kent. It is thanks to the late Francis Pickett that so many people today in Great Britain have easy access to this proven herbal remedy (in the form of Rutivite tablets or green buckwheat tea) to which he himself felt he owed the last 15 years of his life, and the story of this intriguing herbal remedy, and how it can help *you*, makes very interesting reading.

1.

The Rutin Story

How It All Began . . .

This is the fascinating story of how a small amount of buckwheat, brought to this country from North America over 40 years ago to speed a single man's recovery from a serious illness, has blossomed into a thriving business, distributing several tonnes of an intriguing herbal remedy every year and helping to restore many, many happy users to health.

For some time during the Second World War, Francis Pickett was heavily involved with installing retractable gun-turrets or pill-boxes to defend aerodromes against the low-flying aircraft, which had been destroying our own aircraft before they could become airborne — his own invention, in fact. Then in 1942, wracked by overwork, Francis Pickett suffered a stroke. The strain and stress of working such long hours was compounded by incorrect diet leading to very high blood pressure. The only known remedies at the time were strict diet, sedatives and rest, but, by great good fortune, Francis Pickett came to hear about the beneficial effect of a substance called rutin which was a flavonoid extracted from various plants and trees.

Scientists at the Eastern Regional Research Laboratory of the United States Department of Agriculture had confirmed, after hundreds of experiments, that rutin causes blood vessels to become more flexible and overcomes capillary fragility. This helped to protect the body against strokes, and problems of weakened blood vessels caused by X-rays. Rutin was given to American servicemen and other personnel who might have suffered from internal haemorrhage caused by contact with atomic fission products and the effects of atomic radiation around this time.

At first, friends in America sent rutin pills to Francis Pickett, but then exchange controls prevented the purchase of further supplied. One of the main commercially viable sources of rutin is buckwheat, so in 1947 he decided to grow buckwheat on his farm in Kent and dry it in small quantities in a hop kiln, and began to produce a herbal tea in a modest way from the dried leaves and flowers. His health improved as he continued to drink a glassful of an infusion of green buckwheat tea every day and his wife added a little to every pot of ordinary tea that she made, too. Word about the excellent effects of this treatment spread and many friends and acquaintances with similar problems wanted to try it.

With the help of a friend, the Picketts started a small mail order business, much of which was built up by personal recommendations and word of mouth, and they were very happy to see how many of their invalid friends steadily regained health and vigour, often adding ten or more years to their expected lifespan. Later, they went into partnership with Jack Rudkin and formed a new marketing company called Rutin Products, of which Jack Rudkin became chief executive. Sales have risen from a few hundredweight in 1952 to many tonnes per year and are still increasing.

Francis Pickett died in 1957 at the age of 72, convinced that he owed the last 15 years of his life to rutin's remarkable effects. His family continue to produce the buckwheat in

Kent, now using special driers and processes to cope with the large quantities required, but, even today, it is a family-run business producing purely herbal products, including Green Buckwheat Tea and Rutivite tablets made from the ground and compressed leaves and flowers of buckwheat.

2.
Harvest Time On The Farm

Alan Pickett took over in 1957 as grower, and chairman of the marketing company, and instituted comprehensive trials to find the most efficient ways of growing, harvesting and drying the precious crop of buckwheat. In 1966, a large continuous drier was installed which enabled production to climb from the previous two tonnes per year to ten tonnes and more. The possible problems of overheating the crop in this part of the production process meant that a very accurate temperature control was required. A new continuous sifting plant to separate the stalks from leaves and flowers efficiently and speedily was also necessary.

Drying at the point of harvest, as they do in Kent, produces a crop impervious to atmospheric moisture which would destroy the rutin content. Once the dried leaf and flower has been packed and sealed, it keeps indefinitely, whatever the climate. The preparation of buckwheat in Britain has improved greatly in the past few years, resulting in higher yields, with an increase in the rutin content of the dried buckwheat leaf, which is now well above the best-recorded American crop.

After the buckwheat has been cut in the field, it is mechanically loaded on to tractor-mounted stillages or platforms. It is then transported to the feed end of the continuous belt, which moves the buckwheat into the tunnel drier and then it goes through the sifting machine. Close inspection follows, providing maximum quality control. All the green leaf is graded and inspected before being packed into moisture-proof bags ready for shipment all over the world.

Some of the tea is packaged in small cartons ready for marketing and the rest is sent for grinding and compressing into tablets, for those who find it easier and more palatable to add them to ordinary tea or carry them about and take when required.

Buckwheat was selected for its high rutin and mineral content — it also has appreciable amounts of calcium, potassium, magnesium, iron and trace elements as well as some protein and chlorophyll. Almost all the rutin and goodly amounts of the minerals are extracted by boiling water in the normal manner of making tea.

A noticeable improvement in health should be experienced once the blood vessels begin to become more flexible and elastic, which usually happens after several weeks of taking rutin. As rutin seems to have a tonic effect on the entire system, some benefit may be noticed in as little as a week, as a feeling of increased well-being. It is particularly valuable to middle-aged men and women to counter the effects of hardening of the arteries and blood vessels. Rutin improves the circulation, so it is used by many elderly people who suffer from cold hands and feet. It has also proved to be an excellent cure for chilblains for this reason.

The harvest may be over for the year in the Kent acres but it is only just beginning for us for we can now look forward to taking a harvest of health into our daily lives.

3.
What Is Rutin?

Experiments carried out since 1936 have shown the existence of another factor in addition to vitamin C in the juice and rind of citrus fruits and elsewhere. In 1936, Albert Szent-Gyorgyi in Hungary found certain therapeutic qualities in paprika which cured a case of blood vessel bleeding, and in 1939 H. Scarborough in Scotland reported clinical evidence for the existence of a substance which decreased capillary fragility. This was then named vitamin P (for permeability as this substance stabilized the permeability of blood vessels and referred to the ability of a liquid to pass through a structure without affecting it injuriously) and is now known as hesperidin, of which rutin is a very close chemical relative sharing its ability to regulate the permeability of the capillaries thus helping to prevent haemorrhages and ruptures. Scarborough demonstrated vitamin P deficiency in man and showed the difference between its haemorrhagic symptoms and those due to scurvy which is caused by a deficiency of vitamin C itself.

"Vitamin P was an example of serendipity," wrote Albert Szent-Gyorgyi although, as he pointed out later . . . "American science did not take in a friendly spirit to vitamin P and the name 'vitamin' was dropped. I think this is due to the fact that in the USA citrus fruits belong to people's regular daily diet. They are rich in flavones, so a lack of flavones is very rare and if there is no deficiency, a vitamin has no action. In contrast to this, in countries where citrus fruits are expensive, the lack of flavones may cause trouble and their medication may show favourable effects." Albert Szent-Gyorgyi concludes ". . . while these discussions were going on, important experimental material was collected in Hungary which, to my mind, leaves no doubt about the vitamin nature and the biological action of flavones."

It is not now, however, thought to be a vitamin in the true sense of the word but to be the bioflavonoid part of vitamin C. The bioflavonoids are a simple combination of brightly-coloured natural substances which are water-soluble and often appear in fruits and vegetables as companions to vitamin C and their absorption and storage properties are very similar. The bioflavonoids consist of rutin, hesperidin, citrin, the flavones and flavonals. Although rutin is only part of vitamin P, it seems to be the major part and the name is often used synonymously.

During the two World Wars, the herb rue, from which rutin takes its name, was the cheapest and most easily available source of rutin and it was used to thin the viscosity of the blood and encourage the expulsion of fluid from the body tissues — in other words, to act as a diuretic. Herbalists believe rue to have an amazing affinity for the circulatory system and use it to treat their patients for associated problems. Rue contains rutosides and belongs to the *rutaceae* family which, not surprisingly, includes the citrus fruits.

It was then found that rutin also contributed to a drop in blood pressure and it is now frequently used for this purpose. During the Second World War, three eminent Plant Chemistry Scientists in America, J. Q. Griffith Jr, J. F. Couch and M. A. Lindauer, ran clinical trials which showed that rutin had amazing powers to prevent internal haemorrhage caused by radioactivity. Rutin was then given to the civilian and military personnel involved in atomic fission tests as a prophylactic (preventive agent) to help strengthen the capillaries to resist the dangerous effects.

Where Is It Found?

Rutin is found throughout the plant kingdom in berry fruits such as blackcurrants, cherries, grapes, plums, strawberries, citrus fruits (it is contained in the white pith just underneath the skin), but especially in the leaves and flowers of buckwheat, tobacco leaves, in elder flowers, violet and forsythia. Investigations showed that buckwheat was the best source of rutin for medicinal purposes. It has been grown successfully in the green fields of Kent over the past 40 years. It yields all the requirements for what is happily termed "a harvest of health for many".

The name buckwheat may have been taken from the Scandinavian word for beech which is *boc* (for the shape of the grain resembles a beechnut) or it may be a corruption of *Boek-weit,* the Dutch form of the name meaning "Beech-wheat", a translation of the Latin name *Fagopyrum* (Latin *fagus,* a beech).

4.

Can Rutin Help You?

Alternative medicine offers an answer to a number of bodily ailments with this safe, effective and proven herbal remedy. Professor J. B. Harborne at the Department of Botany, Reading University, says: "If you take rutin tablets you are assuring yourself that your body is receiving adequate flavonoids which may be generally beneficial to your health, particularly in relation to high blood pressure."

This confirms that rutin therapy works in helping the many who suffer from high blood pressure, which is often a result of hypertension, and it has also been applied successfully in the treatment of many other ailments which are briefly covered here.

Fragile capillaries are more common than people realise and several weeks of treatment with the bioflavonoids, especially in combination with vitamin C, can improve capillary strength dramatically. Capillaries are the tiniest blood vessels — it would take over a thousand placed side by side to measure a centimetre in width — and they have the vital task of passing food from the bloodstream into the cells and tissues, and collecting waste products from the tissues ready for removal from the body. Thus it is not difficult to see why the well-being of these microscopic blood vessels is of the utmost importance to bodily health and why helping them to function efficiently can aid so many illnesses. These capillaries should be strong and elastic and the bioflavonoids are vital to health because of their beneficial action on this myriad of minute blood vessels.

A series of papers written by John Q. Griffith Jr, MD and Charles F. Krewson Naghski, Ph.D., offers a revealing insight into how scientific tests proved that rutin can do amazing things to help sufferers from the effects of haemorrhages, the prevention of thrombosis, and those with radiation haemorrhages. Exposure of patients to X-rays can weaken the tiny veins and arteries in any part of the body, so this is another problem where rutin can be of use. Rutin is also given as a precautionary measure to dental patients if a tendency towards increased bleeding is suspected, as it reduces clotting time. But rutin is used especially as an internal medicine to treat essential and nephrogenic hypertonia — even before a rise in blood pressure. The first symptom of trouble is a change in the capillaries of the kidneys which restricts the blood supply so that the kidneys themselves may be damaged — and in order to prevent retinal and cerebral haemorrhages, and thus apoplexy, by increasing capillary resistance. Vascular incidents for sufferers of arteriosclerosis are thus prevented. In the early stages of arterial high blood pressure, capillary injury is found in the brain as well as the kidneys. It should be noted that those with increased capillary fragility are especially predisposed to apoplexy, retinal and cerebral haemorrhage.

Rutin has proved to be especially helpful in preventing recurrent bleeding caused by weakened blood vessels, so it has been used in the treatment of haemorrhoids and varicose veins, for example, as it helps to prevent the blood vessel walls from becoming fragile.

Rutin has also been administered successfully in the

treatment of non-tubercular lung haemorrhages, ulcerative colitis and enteritis, nephritis with capillary fragility and as a guard against haemorrhages caused by overdosage with the drug Dicoumarol — an oral anticoagulant used to prevent blood clots for which an initial large dosage is given because of its delayed action which sometimes causes a haemorrhage. For this reason it has now largely been replaced by more controllable drugs.

Rutin has also been found useful as an antihistamine. Histamine is a chemical substance which occurs naturally in the body tissues and, in small amounts, it has many far-reaching actions on muscles, blood capillaries (which it causes to enlarge, increasing the bloodflow in the tissue) and gastric secretions. Sometimes, large amounts of histamine are released with irritating or possibly dangerous results. Excessive amounts of histamine may dilate the small blood vessels to such an extent that they leak blood into the surrounding tissues causing the redness and swelling called inflammation. Thus released in sudden large amounts, histamine can cause allergic reactions, as in asthma for example. Broken capillaries may permit other foreign or incompletely digested food substances to enter the bloodstream where they act as poisons and so result in other allergic reactions.

In purpura, blood transfers spontaneously from capillaries into the skin appearing as small red spots or large plaques, or oozes to or from the mucous membranes. This may be caused by impaired function of the capillary walls or defective quality or quantity of the blood platelets — a situation where rutin has beneficial effects — and may appear as a result of various conditions.

Angina pectoris, characterised by severe pain in the heart

region, is caused by poor blood supply to the heart tissue resulting in a lack of oxygen. Arteriosclerosis, or hardening of the arteries that supply the heart with blood, is the usual cause.

There are several schools of thought on the cause of arteriosclerosis, a related condition, but it may be the result of a metabolic defect involving fats. Fat molecules are usually absorbed through the artery walls and an excess will restrict bloodflow by causing the artery walls to thicken and plaques of cholesterol to narrow the arteries. The artery walls lose their natural elasticity, becoming hard and brittle, and small vessels beneath the plaques may haemorrhage, causing cholesterol deposits to break free, or a blood clot may form. Either or both of these conditions may conspire to block the blood vessel with symptoms similar to those of a heart attack but lasting only a few minutes. If the blood supply is decreased sufficiently, however, this condition can progress to a heart attack with sometimes fatal results.

A "stroke", or cerebrovascular accident, occurs when the blood supply to an area of brain cells is cut off for a lengthy period so that the deprived cells die from lack of oxygen and nutrients essential to the brain's function. The cause of the blood vessel blockage may be atherosclerosis, clotting or haemorrhaging, and one of the predisposing factors is prolonged high blood pressure, for which rutin is especially recommended. Rutin helps to maintain a healthy circulatory system and ensure flexible, elastic blood vessel walls, especially of the capillaries.

This action is also vital in preventing the problems associated with the development of arthritis. If internal haemorrhages occur through weakened capillaries, they have serious repercussions because cells beyond the break cease to receive vital nourishment and die. This provides the ideal feeding ground for bacteria so that they begin to multiply, their enzyme action produces toxins and the area becomes infected and inflamed. This often happens at much-used parts of the body such as particular joints, and may result in painful crippling, swelling and loss of movement as the condition deteriorates. Rheumatic fever and bursitis may also benefit from bioflavonoid treatment.

A capillary-strengthening action can show its benefits in many parts of the body. The eye, for example, is a very sensitive organ and someone skilled at reading its condition such as an iridologist can see signs of many physical ailments and nutritional deficiencies there. Rutin may help many eye diseases, even glaucoma, because this is caused by fluid build-up and engorgement of the blood vessels. In diabetics, broken capillaries and blood oozing in the retina is quite commonly seen — all diabetics with high blood pressure show extreme capillary fragility. This weakened capillary condition seems frequently to be the cause of internal bleeding.

The bioflavonoids have also been helpful in cases of haemophilia which is an hereditary blood disease characterized by a prolonged coagulation time — blood fails to clot and abnormal bleeding occurs.

Restless Legs and Rutin
An inability to keep the legs still or an itching, burning or prickling, usually in the lower leg area, are aggravating features of the so-called "restless legs" syndrome. This is an early manifestation of chronic venous insufficiency and is associated with the development of small perforating veins in the lower leg which are eventually unable to support the high pressure of blood to be pumped back to the heart. Pressure in the

capillaries causes fluid leakage in the surrounding tissues, leading to oedema of legs and ankles. Poor oxygen supply to the tissues then results in a heavy feeling in the legs when standing and, when lying down, restlessness and night cramps which disturb sleep. The eventual result would be the development of venous ulcers but, fortunately, rutin has well-proven beneficial effects on capillary permeability and is known to improve circulation.

Chilblains — reddening, swelling and itching which can occur on fingers, toes, ears or nose — benefit greatly from improved circulation which is worth bearing in mind when the cold weather comes.

Symptoms of leukaemia include bleeding from gums, nose, stomach and rectum and abnormally easy and excessive bruising of the skin: rutin has been used to help alleviate these distressing problems.

Pyorrhoea, an infectious disease of the gums and tooth sockets with the formation of pus and usually loosening of teeth, and gum disorders such as puffiness, tenderness, soreness and bleeding, are often related to vitamin C and bioflavonoid deficiencies which cause increased capillary fragility. Citrus fruits have a long-held reputation for preventing scurvy through their vitamin C content but they were also known to decrease the capillary fragility signalled by bleeding gums and other symptoms of this deficiency disease, demonstrating the useful effect of the bioflavonoids. In fact, the body's utilisation of vitamin C is improved when the bioflavonoids are present.

It can plainly be seen that the application of rutin to a wide range of such bodily ailments can have wonderfully healing results and its possible benefits cannot be ignored in its life-enhancing effects.

The major application of rutin's ability to normalise high blood pressure is covered separately in greater detail.

5.

The Drawbacks of
Drug Treatment

Contrast such benefits to the body from a herbal treatment
free from side-effects with the many possible drawbacks of
drug treatment bearing in mind their speedy and perhaps
temporary results.

It is most important to look with great caution at some
of the "wonder drugs" that have, in the past decade, been
heralded as "sure cures" for hypertension and circulatory
disorders.

The use of these drugs in large doses has sometimes,
however, resulted in fatalities and even where average dosage
is taken, these drugs should not be used for any length of
time — possibly no longer than a few weeks. An increasing
number of doctors are becoming aware that so many drugs
neither cure nor offer lasting benefit to sufferers.

Medical evidence shows all too clearly that the complete
answer to treating high blood pressure has not yet been found.
Drugs, however positive their action may be in helping
sufferers from hypertension itself, have a number of possible
side-effects listed against their names in medical reference
books and some of these warnings make far from cheerful
reading.

For example, the vasodilator anti-hypertensive drug
Diazoxide has a number of possible adverse effects including
fluid and salt retention for which a diuretic may have to be

given, blood disorders, interference with growth in children, tachycardia (rapid heartbeat) and hyperglycaemia (excess sugar in the blood).

Hydrallazine hydrochloride (Apresoline) in the same drug category, lists nausea, vomiting, rapid heartbeat, flushing, sweating, pins and needles, numbness in hands and feet, trembling, breathlessness, skin rashes and depression, usually in the first weeks of treatment. Prolonged use may produce the symptoms of rheumatoid arthritis or systemic lupus erythaematosus (this affects the connective tissue and may involve the joints, lungs, heart, kidney or skin with pain in the joints, muscles, or abdomen). Minoxdil quotes gastro-intestinal disturbances, weight gain, peripheral oedema, tachycardia, and breast tenderness as possible side-effects, and an alarming caution that the first dose may cause loss of consciousness for up to one hour! Lower dosages can cause renal failure and doctors are advised to avoid withdrawing the drug abruptly.

Recent revelations disclose that Inderal (Propranol), as well as being inclined to induce asthma, can also encourage wet dreams. As a doctor explained to me, it is a bitter-sweet story when this drug gives a man such a strong desire for his partner that a heart attack may be induced by excessive physical activity. The very pill he takes to revive himself may thus lead to a complete decline in his condition. This "urge that kills' is said by the medical profession to be "not uncommon".

The so-called "wonder drug" Eraldin (Practolol) had to be withdrawn from general prescription and is now restricted to emergency use only through the occurrence of a serious adverse reaction syndrome following long-term oral use. These included painful eye damage, even causing blindness in some rare cases; peritonitis; deafness and, in rare instances, a severe inflammatory disease called lupus erythaematosus causing scaly red patches on the skin, and another due to fibrous tissue formation called Peyronie's Disease, which can cause serious and painful sexual difficulties for men.

An unpleasant side-effect of beta-blockers is miserably disturbed nights by nightmares. Tests have shown that Propranolol, Metoprolol and Pindolol have a detrimental effect on sleep patterns. The chemical structures of these particular drugs gives them an affinity for fats and it is thought that, because of this, they can more easily seep into the central nervous system which is protected by a fatty layer and so have a direct effect on the brain.

I could go on, of course, but isn't this alone sufficient reason for a patient wishing to choose a safe herbal medicine, instead? For even if the beneficial effects *do* take longer to appear, who would want an "instant" cure when all one really gets is a lifetime of side-effects, for often the damage done to a patient can take a long time to repair.

Letters from many anxious hypertension sufferers mention a number of different drugs being prescribed for one condition. One 48-year-old woman suffering from hypertension was prescribed two Navidrex K tablets each morning (a diuretic), Betoloc 100mg, twice a day (a beta-blocker used to treat angina and raised blood pressure) and Apresoline (see pg. 28), one three times a day.

Her worried husband enquired about Rutivite, asking if it would be harmful to take along with this prescription. This is just where a natural product like Rutivite can help a sufferer to reduce drug dosage once the side-effects that a longterm drug regime may induce are becoming apparent. A herbal medicine may be slower in its action but will actually help the body to heal itself instead of just masking the symptoms.

But how dependent on drugs can the body become? Alas, very dependent. And it is only by gradually reducing the drug intake and backing it up with a herbal remedy like Rutivite that the first real step towards helping the body to heal itself naturally will be achieved.

6.

Herbal Help For High Blood Pressure

Rutin's most widely recognized value is in helping those who suffer from hypertension or high blood pressure — a chronic condition which, along with ailments like migraine and backache make it well-suited to a new medical approach and one in which rutin can play an active and vital part.

The British Heart Foundation in their Heart Research Series say that, taken literally, hypertension means no more than "increased tension". In medical terminology this implies that the pressure exerted by the heart in its task of forcing blood through the circulation has become excessive, although there is no universal agreement on the upper limits of what is considered normal, especially with increasing age. Blood pressure increases about one degree in every two years — normal at 30 years of age is about 125 and at 60, 140. Those who are physically weak have a slightly lower degree and it will increase a little with exercise. If blood pressure is too high or too low, then something is wrong with the circulation.

Blood Circulation
Blood circulation is the flow of blood in the blood vessels throughout the body and it is kept up by the constant rhythmic contractions and pumping action of the heart.

The lungs are collapsed and do not begin to function until a child is born, so that very often the newborn infant has to be slapped to make him start breathing. The heart, on the other hand, begins its life-long task early in foetal development and continues its faithful work all through life.

At the same time that the heart and blood vessels are developing in the embryo, blood and blood cells are produced by the same embryonic cell formation called blood islands. This comparatively poor and primitive circulatory system gets its oxygen and nutriments from the mother's circulation, and also disposes of its oxidation products into the mother's blood. The two systems communicate in the structure of the placenta (afterbirth) through the navel and umbilical cord. As soon as the infant is born and the connection is severed at the navel, the child begins to use its own lungs, getting oxygen from the air and food as received.

As soon as the newborn infant re-routes its circulation to conform to its new way of life, the blood vessels leading from the navel become shrivelled and, in time, obliterated and the extra opening (foramen ovale) between the two upper chambers (atria) of the heart closes up and disappears. If, as sometimes happens, this opening fails to close, a "blue baby" is the result.

The course of the newborn infant's circulation, which remains the same throughout life, is thus: the fresh, red oxygenated blood coming from the lungs through the pulmonary veins is delivered into the left upper chamber of the heart (left atrium); from there it flows into the powerful lower left chamber (left ventricle), which contracts strongly and forces its contents into the main artery (aorta). Being elastic like all arteries, the aorta transmits the propulsive force of the heart throughout its branches and their capillaries (capillaries are the final link between the blood and body tissues, carrying substances to and from the larger blood vessels), distributing good blood to every part of the body, giving oxygen and nourishment to every body cell. On its return course, the impoverished blood gathers all waste material, becoming dark and purplish as it flows back via the small veins from every part of the body, until it finally reaches the largest vein (vena cava) and is delivered to the right atrium of the heart.

This part of the circulation, performed by the left side of the heart, is termed the "greater" or "systemic" circulation. It performs the colossal task of servicing the entire body machinery with pure life-giving blood.

The impure blood brought back by the veins passes from the right atrium to the right ventricle, which contracts and forces it into a large artery (the pulmonary artery), which branches out to both lungs where the blood gives up some of its impurities as carbon dioxide (other impurities are extracted by the kidneys), and takes on a fresh supply of oxygen. The refreshed blood completes the trip via the pulmonary veins to the left atrium, as mentioned before. Pumping of the impure blood by the right side of the heart through the lungs is called the "lesser" or "pulmonary" circulation.

The right and left sides of the heart act in unison. One volume of blood makes the entire circuit and is returned to the same point in the heart within eight-tenths of a second. Of this, around one-tenth of a second is taken up by the contraction of the atria and three-tenths by contraction of the ventricles (together called the "systolic" or "active" phase). The remaining four-tenths of a second are used by the heart as a rest period (the diastolic phase). During that time, all four chambers of the heart are quiescent and the heart recoups itself for the next contraction which follows promptly, timed to the fraction of a second.

Heartbeat is a term that can be applied correctly only to the forceful contractions of the heart ventricles. You can feel the heart beat on the left side of the chest, a little inside and below the left nipple. The pointed tip of the left ventricle comes very close to the chest wall so that you sense its powerful contractions. With the heart contracting approximately once in eight-tenths of a second, it follows that in one minute the heart will beat around 75 times. A healthy adult's pulse rate at rest is about 65-80 a minute with women tending to be in the upper range. Children have a higher rate — as much as 140 in an infant.

The propulsion of the blood into the elastic arteries every time the heart beats is what makes the pulse, which you can feel at the wrist or in any other part of the body where an artery is near enough to the surface. The pulse corresponds to the heartbeat: when your heart works faster, the pulse is faster. The faster you work a machine, the sooner it wears out and the heart is affected in the same way. Overwork, overexcitement, too much exercise, heavy eating or drinking, cause the heart to become strained and to wear out prematurely.

Recently, doctors at a Birmingham hospital have discovered that, with some people, even quite moderate drinking habits (no more than 10 pints of beer a week, for example) can cause blood pressure to rise sufficiently to increase greatly the risk of heart attacks and strokes. They advise a limit of either two pints of beer, two measures of spirit or three glasses of wine a day, although this may still be too high for safety for some people.

Blood Pressure

The forceful impact produced by the powerful contraction

of the heart muscle, especially the left ventricle, is called blood pressure. It is transmitted to the blood vessels by the volume of blood thrown into them with every heart contraction. This force can be measured and recorded by an apparatus called a sphygmanometer.

Generally speaking, an increase in the blood pressure is an indication that the heart is working against some increased resistance, the cause of which may be a loss of elasticity or hardening of the arteries (arteriosclerosis) incident to age and other causes, or the resistance may be caused by disease in some important organ such as the kidneys or liver, thereby obstructing the flow of blood through that organ and resulting in resistance to the heart's action, increasing the force of its contractions and thereby raising the blood pressure.

Blood pressure varies greatly in different individuals under normal conditions — it can, for example, be 110 or less in one and 140 or 150 in another. Two types of pressure are measured with the sphygmanometer. The *systolic* pressure is the pressure in the blood vessels when the heart contracts and pumps the blood — this is the higher figure. The *diastolic* pressure is the blood pressure when the heart relaxes. The results are then expressed as two figures, e.g. 120/80, which might be the pressure of the average young person. A middle-aged person may have a systolic pressure of around 145 and a diastolic pressure of 90. A systolic pressure of 160 and diastolic pressure of 90 may indicate high blood pressure.

Normal blood pressure is maintained by:

1.   The contraction and pumping action of the heart.
2.   Elasticity of the blood vessel walls.
3.   The resistance in the minute blood vessels.
4.   The volume of blood.

5.   Thickness or viscosity of the blood.
6.   The amount of adrenal gland secretion. (These are a
     pair of endocrine glands situated at the top of the kidneys
     which secrete a number of hormones into the
     bloodstream, including adrenaline and cortisol which
     influence many bodily processes.)

The heart's normal pumping action generates enough
pressure to force blood and fluid around the circulation; in
high blood pressure this is too high for the body's normal
needs which puts the heart under strain as it has to pump
harder to get the blood round the body. It also gradually
damages the small blood vessels in the kidneys and eyes.

It is the blood pressure which forces oxygen and food, or
plasma carrying sugar, amino acids, fatty acids, vitamins and
minerals into the tissues through porous microscopic capillary
walls; hence normal blood pressure is vital to the nutrition
of cells. When the blood in the capillary beds becomes
concentrated through loss of plasma, the blood protein
albumin attracts tissue fluids carrying wastes into the vessels,
causing the quantity of blood to remain remarkably constant.
Thus, by virtue of the blood pressure, all tissues are constantly
bathed in fresh nutrient-laden fluid and the breakdown
products from worn-out cells are removed.

When larger amounts of oxygen and nutrients are needed,
the contraction of tiny muscles in the arterial walls causes
the pressure to increase and supplies to be pushed more
quickly to the cells; if few nutrients are required, these muscles
relax, pressure decreases and food is conserved.

Blood pressure becomes elevated when larger than normal
amounts of water (and sodium) are held in the body — a
situation which occurs in the alarm reaction to stress. In this

case, the quantity of blood plasma or the blood volume increases. On the other hand, arteries can become smaller when tension causes the muscular walls to contract or when they are plugged by cholesterol, compressed in beds of fat or shrunk by scar tissue that may be calcified. The most persistent high blood pressure results from a combination of these factors.

One of the functions of the kidneys is to control blood pressure. When oxygen is inadequate, they appear to secrete a hormone-like "pressor" factor which elevates the blood pressure, thus increasing the oxygen supply. Because vitamin E decreases the need for oxygen, it is especially important for people with high blood pressure. Deficiencies of choline, or vitamin C or E causes haemorrhages in the kidneys and brings oxygen starvation to cells formerly dependent on the interrupted blood supply — this may elevate blood pressure.

The significance of hypertension lies in its potentially injurious effects upon the arterial circulation, in particular upon the arteries both large and small which provide the circulation to brain, kidneys and heart. By damaging arteries leading to the brain, it may prepare the way for a subsequent slight or major stroke precipitated either by haemorrhage or by clot formation. Strokes and coronary thrombosis are more common in people with high blood pressure and so the old saying that a man is only as good as his blood vessels was never more true than it is today.

Doctors agree that lowering high blood pressure prolongs the expectation of life, as surveys indicate that at least one man in two will show evidence of diseased coronary arteries by the age of 65 years, and that 38 per cent of the 73,000 male deaths between 30 years of age and retirement are attributable to this cause.

However, there may be no symptoms of hypertension in itself apart from occasional headaches and giddiness until shortness of breath from strain on the heart or blurred vision from damage to the retina at the back of the eye occurs. For many people, the first realisation that they are suffering from high blood pressure comes from a routine medical examination for quite another purpose.

Kidney ailments, arteriosclerosis (hardening of the arteries) and other diseases or defects of the circulation, tumours of the adrenal glands and disease of the brain may be responsible for high blood pressure. But a specific cause is found in only about one in ten of all cases. In the remainder, the high blood pressure is described as "essential" or "primary", which simply means that a cause cannot be determined.

But in a large number of cases the onset of hypertension may be associated with heredity, obesity, physical or emotional stress, high salt intake, cigarette smoking, and excessive intake of stimulants such as coffee, tea or drugs.

Stress is an important factor to be considered in hypertension. Many people drive themselves too hard and consequently become hypertensive. These people must learn to avoid stressful conditions by changing their lifestyle. They should take regular, unhurried meals, try to avoid worry, allow themselves plenty of leisure time, take regular holidays and generally use moderation in all things. If one's occupation involves excessive emotional and physical stress, one may have to change it or adjust it to make it less stressful.

Sodium is a primary cause of hypertension because it causes fluid retention, which adds extra stress to heart and circulatory systems. Increasing potassium intake will cause the body to excrete more sodium — potassium-high foods are celery, cucumber, lettuce, cabbage, cauliflower, tomato and watercress. Rutin also acts as a diuretic, causing fluid to be expelled from the tissues.

Vitamin C and the bioflavonoids, including rutin, can help to maintain the health of the blood vessels that are strained by the greater pressure placed on them by hypertension. Regular exercise is essential in preventing high blood pressure because it keeps the circulatory system healthy. Promoting a tranquil outlook on life is of primary importance in reducing and preventing hypertension and this can be aided by relaxation exercises and such activities as yoga.

Extra cholesterol may form fatty deposits clogging artery walls and heart — cholesterol is certainly needed (the body will manufacture it if it is not present) but unless other factors are balanced to handle it, the cholesterol is going to settle in deposits along the internal walls of the heart and its arteries and veins, closing up the pipes that carry blood through the body — then up goes the blood pressure. Lecithin, vitamin E and herbal treatments which include rutin will help to avert such damage.

Rutin or vitamin P is especially valuable to sufferers from high blood pressure for it strengthens and increases the efficiency of the small blood vessels — both the arterioles (the smallest of the arterial vessels) and the venules (the smallest of the veins). If the blood pressure is high, the pipes which carry the blood must be strong and elastic to cope. Rutin can be used as a food supplement in medicinal quantities to help.

Try to change to a new and healthier way of life and let the pure goodness of Rutivite help you. Think of it rather like a New Year's resolution to wipe the slate clean and start life all over again. Make a fresh start and see how much better you can feel!

This applies particularly to those who feel that, because they are no longer young, life holds no more for them. Often the so-called "elderly" are treated rather like sheep in a pen and allow themselves to be forced into accepting the limitations of increasing age. The fact is that some of the drugs which are given to try and help reduce high blood pressure can be dangerous when administered to the elderly and to those who have had a cerebral haemorrhage or suffer from coronary thrombosis.

A sudden fall in blood pressure can be as dangerous as continuing high blood pressure and your doctor should plan your individual treatment with care. If you suffer from the symptoms of high blood pressure such as headache, dizziness and shortness of breath then a drug, sensibly administered, may help these conditions far more than aiming for a dramatic drop in the blood pressure itself.

It is also of vital importance to make sure that you do not suffer from constipation. As far back as 1961, medical investigators found that straining at stool, especially by those who have had heart attacks and suffer from high blood pressure may cause coronary thrombosis or a cerebrovascular accident. A well-planned properly-balanced diet based on plenty of fresh raw fruit, salads, vegetables and wholegrains should make constipation a thing of the past as well as improving health generally, while rutin also has a mildly aperient action.

7.
Diet for Heart and Circulatory Problems

The importance of maintaining a healthy heart and circulatory system never seems to be out of the news these days, and rightly so. The following guidelines have been devised to encourage good heart and cardiovascular health. If you have any worries about pursuing a regime of this kind, refer them to your medical practitioner.

General Points

1. Smoking should be eliminated completely and if this is not possible it should certainly be kept to an absolute minimum. The heart, cardiovascular system and many other systems and organs, are all under much greater strain when they have to cope with the longterm and destructive habit of smoking. So, for your health's sake, don't!
2. Regular exercise is a must. This should preferably be outdoor exercise in clean, fresh air. If this is not possible, an indoor exercise regime must suffice. It is important to exercise regularly as it is better to exercise four times per week every week, than seven times in the first week and then take no exercise at all for the next few weeks. Choose an exercise programme that suits you and your individual preferences and remember to build up your programme gradually as your fitness level increases.

3. Everyone has stresses and worries, but it is how you handle them that is important. Another major key to a healthy life which will help you to avoid coronaries and other major problems is to learn to handle stresses and worries effectively. Stress may be physical or mental. Physical stresses can include lead leaking into the water supply from old lead plumbing, excessive intake of aluminium through the use of aluminium cooking utensils, and an overload of other toxic metals in the body from various environmental and work sources. These stresses should be dealt with by following a specific detoxification programme.

   Mental stresses should be dealt with by cultivating a positive and constructive mental outlook, and here meditation and relaxation exercises can be most helpful. The importance of sufficient rest and a good night's sleep to refresh and restore body, mind and spirit cannot be too strongly emphasized.

4. Attention to attaining and maintaining normal weight levels is also important. Those who are overweight must reduce the extra strain on their heart and cardiovascular system by gradually and sensibly bringing their weight down to normal.

Diet Pointers

1. Attention to fat intake is most important. Ideally, the diet should contain as little animal fat as possible, and even lean meat should be kept to a minimum with protein coming from vegetable and dairy food sources for preference. Fried food (especially deep-fried) should be omitted completely and on no account should animal fats of any description (e.g. lard, dripping) be used for

cooking. This is because animal fats contain saturated fatty acids which, in many cases, are a major contributory factor to a state encouraging the development of heart disease, arteriosclerosis, etc.

It is, however, most important that the diet should contain a plentiful supply of unsaturated fatty acids, best obtained from pure vegetable oils. The best sources are sunflower seed oil, safflower seed oil, soya bean oil and olive oil. Make sure that these oils are of the finest quality and not rancid — ideally, cold-pressed should be used.

2. Salt should be excluded from the diet, so avoid adding salt during cooking and after. If this proves difficult, try one of the alternatives such as potassium chloride salt (i.e. Biosalt). Herbs and other flavourings such as Cayenne pepper in moderation can be used to give extra zest to food.

3. Avoid all refined and over-processed foods, especially those containing white flour and white sugar. Consumption of these foods is largely a matter of habit and so-called "convenience" and you will not miss them or feel hungry if you follow the diet recommended here which is health-giving, unlike the all-too-frequent health-robbing diet with its emphasis on carbohydrates, refined sugars and animal protein. Coffee and alcohol should also be severely limited or cut out altogether. Very weak good quality tea, buckwheat tea, other herb teas, dandelion coffee and other cereal-based coffees, dilute fruit and vegetable juices, and bottled spring water offer a wealth of health-building alternatives.

4. This diet emphasises high-quality, natural, raw, live foods and whole grains with their abundance of health-giving

and health-restoring vitamins, minerals, amino acids, enzymes and trace elements.

A recommended list of foods follows and by eating a good variety every day and using a little imagination (there are many very good wholefood recipe books available now), health will be restored or maintained in a most pleasant and varied way and you will feel and look full of verve and vitality.

You May Eat Any of The Following Foods
(Make sure that you include some from each category every day)

Wholegrains: Buckwheat, oats, wheat, barley, corn, millet

Legumes: Soya beans, peas

Nuts: Any in small amounts but especially peanuts (strictly a legume), pecans and black walnuts

Seeds and Oils: Safflower, sunflower, sesame, olive, soya, wheat germ

Vegetables: (raw or baked or lightly steamed to preserve maximum nutrient levels) Garlic, onion, broccoli, Brussels sprouts, cabbage, cauliflower, turnip, greens, spinach, watercress, asparagus, carrots, tomatoes, potato (preferably steamed or baked in jacket), okra, celery, cucumber, endive, parsley, peppers

Fruit: Apple, banana, all citrus — lemon, orange, nectarine, tangerine, grapefruit, etc — pear, peach, pineapple, raspberries, strawberries, cantaloupe, cranberries, guava, mulberries

Protein: Brewer's yeast, cottage cheese, buttermilk, liver, egg yolk in moderation

Drinks: Any of the above fruits and vegetables as juices, particularly citrus and pineapple (remember to dilute for the sake of your teeth); dandelion coffee, buckwheat tea, comfrey tea, rose hip tea especially, and any other herb tea that you like.

Extras: Small amount of margarine, butter, or preferably a nut butter. A little honey.

Supplements: Vitamins B, C, E, P, lecithin, kelp, garlic perles.

A warm bath at night and plenty of sleep in a well-ventilated room will do a great deal to lower blood pressure; hot and cold applications to spine, liver, spleen and stomach; cold towel rubs in the morning on rising; warm baths and salt glows at night; hot and cold showers, are all very helpful. A general massage will help to work waste matter out of the system, equalize the circulation and greatly relieve the burden on heart and nerves.

8.

Questions About Rutivite

Knowledge of the benefits from taking herbal medicines grows daily. People naturally want to know more about herbal remedies so here are some of the queries received about Rutivite and rutin therapy, together with replies provided by the suppliers.

Q. *Do I need to continue taking Rutivite even though my blood pressure is now stable?*

A. Rutivite will help to keep your blood pressure at a stable level if you continue to take it.

Q. *Will it cause any harm if I continue taking the Rutivite tablets or Green Buckwheat Tea?*

A. No, it will not cause any problems if you continue taking Rutivite. In fact, it will do you nothing but good.

Q. *Can the changes which Rutivite makes within the blood circulation, etc, go too far and cause other problems?*

A. Rutivite does not change the blood circulation. It helps to heal the body so it does not cause any unwarranted changes. It merely helps the blood vessels to become more flexible.

Q. *Has Rutivite any specific reaction in cases of pancreatic insufficiency and sugar imbalance?*

A. We cannot guarantee that there will be no reaction. We

suggest that you take some and watch for reactions. A small quantity can be supplied for this purpose if required but if any reaction is likely to do you harm, consult your health practitioner first.

Q. *Can Rutivite be taken with phenobarbitone or other drugs prescribed by my practitioner?*

A. Yes. Rutin is the most placid of substances and we have never yet heard of a drug with which it is not compatible. If you notice no reaction, and it is extremely unlikely that there will be one, you can proceed with the treatment, but if you have any doubts consult a qualified health practitioner. We would not wish you to take our advice if it conflicts with that of any qualified person who has examined you.

Q. *Has rutin a slightly diuretic or aperient effect?*

A. In a few cases it does for reasons which are not clear. It is probably caused by the toning up of the system generally but, in any case, this action should be beneficial to your bodily condition.

Q. *Can rutin help low blood pressure?*

A. No. We have had letters saying that it has but this is possibly because there has been a general improvement in health from the known tonic effect of rutin on the system generally.

Q. *Can it be mixed with maté or peppermint tea?*

A. Yes, if you prefer it that way.

Q. *As it is not convenient for me to make the infusion every day, will it keep if I make enough for a week?*

A. Yes, but do keep it sealed and away from the light,

preferably in a vacuum flask. This idea is not recommended, except when it is unavoidable.

Extracts From Customers' Letters

"I suffer from varicose veins and have been given drugs by my GP to help the circulation in the lower half of my left leg. I am very much against drugs and believe in herbal remedies, I wondered if Rutivite would help me. I took buckwheat tea for high blood pressure when I was pregnant and I must say I also had a very easy childbirth — I have always put it down to the Rutin Tea."

— Mrs J. G. F., Rugby, Warks.

"For the past four years I have tried many products for the relief of my severe varicose veins, including high potencies of lecithin, vitamin E, selenium, etc. Then, last month I tried Rutivite and, to my wonder and disbelief, they have nearly disappeared and the irritation and pain has gone.

These tablets are surely suited to my requirements and I take them with 500 i.u. vitamin E. I look forward to wearing shorts again this summer without the embarrassment of my right leg.

As the manager of a leading health food company, your product is at the top of my list to sell to people with varicose veins and poor circulation. Well done, Rutivite!"

— R. B.

* Factors that inhibit blood circulation increase susceptibility to varicose veins so Rutivite should indeed be helpful in these cases.

"My 17 year-old daughter suffers badly from chilblains from October to February. As this is a circulation problem, could

you please advise me as to whether any of your products would be suitable as treatment."

— Mrs M. W., Purley, Surrey

* Rutivite helps chilblain sufferers to keep the circulation going on the extremities during this troublesome time of year.

"I am interested in taking your buckwheat tablets for high blood pressure. I intend to take them in addition to what I am already taking, which is Trandate, Apresoline and Bendroflozine. As your tablets are made purely from buckwheat, is it necessary to consult my GP?"

— M. R. G., Southport, Merseyside

* It is best to consult your doctor about all the tablets you may take even if they are naturally-based products and not chemically-based drugs. Rutivite, being a product made from natural ingredients, may take a little longer to work but it is better in the long run as it has no side-effects.

Many sufferers from angina and high blood pressure who have, in some cases, been forced to retire early through their illness, write to ask about the safety of taking Rutivite tablets, often alongside such formidable drugs as Inderal (Propranolol) and Diumide K.

"I asked my doctor if I could try once more to live without drugs. My doctor agreed, provided I had weekly check-ups for high blood pressure. The side-effects were unpleasant as I suffered from bad drug withdrawal symptoms but I persevered. I am trying hard to fight a lifetime of drug dependency by taking Rutivite instead, which is slower-acting but has no side-effects."

— Mrs D. J., South Humberside

"I have suffered from fainting fits in Church caused by the action

of drug medication. Will Rutivite help? Many of my friends take it and find it very helpful."

— Mrs C., Wigan, Lancs.

"My doctor says he knows nothing about herbal medicines and refuses to say if I can take Rutivite tablets."

— Mrs L., Rhondda

* Rutivite is prescribed by many doctors throughout the country and will not affect the drugs already supplied. It is surely better to take a safe herbal medicine and aim, where possible, to reduce your intake of modern so-called "wonder drugs".

"I would like further details of your Rutivite tablets as it appears there may be certain circumstances (judging by the warning printed on the label) in which they may do some harm, perhaps to the digestion. My blood pressure is described by my GP as 'on the high side of normal', and he is not giving me anything for it, but if your tablets cannot do any harm, then I should like to try them. Once I start to take them, must I continue to do so in order to avoid any harm?

— J. F. R., Worcester Park, Surrey

* The warning on the Rutivite label is to tell you that you should let your doctor know if you think you have any problems such as high blood pressure, varicose veins and hardening of the arteries, and also should explain to him that you would prefer, if possible, to take Rutivite tablets rather than a prescribed drug. Rutivite will not harm the digestion in any way — it will only deal with the particular problem of your high blood pressure. You are not committed to taking Rutivite forever, but it will be helpful if you take a small maintenance dose to keep your high blood pressure at bay.

The tablets are not addictive like some drugs, so you can stop taking them at any time. They do not have any bad side-effects as they are a totally natural product.

The experience of all investigators who had studied the pharmacology of the flavonoids has indicated their lack of toxicity. The clinical experience of physicians who have had patients on rutin for prolonged periods of time indicates that the drug is non-toxic to man. Some of the patients have been on rutin for up to five years with a daily intake of 60mg or more. All of this data furnishes convincing proof that rutin in innocuous.

"As an assistant in a health food store, I should like some advice on convincing customers that Rutivite may well have advantages over other rutin tablets. Rutivite tablets have been recommended to me in the past by a naturopath and probably for this reason I believe that they have some virtue not possessed by others. However, the price difference between Rutivite tablets and rutin tablets produced by other firms means that some reassurance needs to be given to customers.

— Mrs T. P., Ventnor, I.o.W.

* We think the main point to make is that Rutivite tablets are made purely with genuine Kentish buckwheat leaf and flowers but that no one seems to know exactly what the less expensive ones contain. We have them analysed from time to time and have found that they contain plant matter of an indeterminate nature to which is added the cheaper synthetic rutin. Because of their names, one gets the immediate impression that the products are 100% natural buckwheat but if you check them thoroughly you will find that this is not so.

You will notice that even the least expensive herbal

remedies nearly all cost more than the other less expensive rutin tablets but that is, of course, because of the cheaper materials used in the other brands.

Compare the following points:

Rutivite	Cheaper brands
Is licensed and can make claims	?
Is made from best Kent buckwheat	?
Has been on the market for 37 years	?
Is Britain's best-selling rutin product	?
Is made only from herbal and natural ingredients	?
Is known to work	?

Cheap imitations mean that you are not benefiting as we would like from the wonders of rutin. A recent analysis of a "so-called" 60mg rutin tablet showed that a large percentage of the tablet was made up of lactose and starch leaving 32mg of rutin compared to Rutivite's 54%. After all, customers are spending their hard-earned money on these tablets and should feel that they are buying only the best.

"Can you please send me several copies of your leaflet about Rutivite. I want to give one to my doctor.

I gradually gave up the Aldomet pills prescribed by my doctor by taking Rutivite as well and eventually got down to one Aldomet per day. I then asked my doctor if I could see what happened if I stopped taking the remaining Aldomet and he agreed. At the next check-up my blood pressure reading was good and since then every time I have been for a check-up my doctor has been pleased with the readings. He asked what else I was taking instead of his prescription and was very interested to hear about Rutivite. He said that whatever it was, it was doing a good job.

9.
Glossary

Apoplexy: This is a stroke caused by a cerebral haemorrhage or by a blood clot blocking a blood vessel supplying the brain. Usually suffered by those who are over 40 and have high blood pressure or *atherosclerosis*.

Arteriosclerosis: The medical name for the condition commonly known as "hardening of the arteries". In the middle and later years the arteries may become less flexible as fatty deposits build up in the arteries, narrowing them and causing the walls to become thicker and less resilient.

Atherosclerosis: Where fatty deposits in an artery may narrow the passageway sufficiently so that bloodflow is seriously restricted.

Atrioventricular Block (AV Block): Blocking of impulses that make the heart retract.

Beta-Blocker: A drug that may be prescribed to protect the heart. Beta-receptor cells receive the mental and physical stress messages from the brain and pass on such instructions to the heart, which then beats faster, and the arteries which narrow to push up the blood pressure. Beta-blocker drugs block these instructions so that the heart continues to beat at a normal rate and the arteries do not narrow, so they are given to those who have suffered a heart attack, high blood pressure, angina or sometimes just for anxiety or palpitations.

Bradycardia: Slow rate of heart contraction resulting in a slow pulse rate.

Bronchospasm: Sudden constriction of bronchial tubes.

Cardiogenic Shock: Shock specifically harming the heart, as in major coronary thrombosis.

Cardiovascular: Pertaining to the heart and blood vessels.

Cerebrovascular: Pertaining to blood vessels of the brain.

Cerebrovascular Accident: Apoplexy caused by embolism, haemorrhage or thrombosis in the brain.

Embolism: Obstruction of a blood vessel by impaction of a solid body (thrombi, fat globules, tumour cells) or an air bubble.

Erythema: Reddening of the skin.

Heart Attack: This occurs if the supply of blood to the heart is cut off, thus increasing restriction of blood flow.

Hemiplegia: Paralysis of one side of the body, usually resulting from a cerebrovascular accident on the opposite side.

Phaeochromocytoma: Rare tumour of the adrenal gland — blood pressure intermittently high in spurts.

Pressor: A substance which raises the blood pressure.

Stroke: Popular term for apoplexy resulting from a vascular accident in the brain, usually resulting in hemiplegia.

Systole: The contraction phase of the cardiac cycle.

Tachycardia: Rapid heartbeat.

Thrombosis: Intravascular formation of a blood clot.

Vasodilator: Any agent which causes widening of the lumen (space inside tubular structure) of blood vessels.

10.
Appendix

Rutin's synonyms are:
- Vitamin P
- Vitamin P factor
- Rutoside
- Quercetin-3-rutinoside
- 3,3' 4'm5,7 - Pentahydroxyflavone-3-rutinoside
- Antipermeability factor

Appearance: Yellow to a matt greenish, crystalline powder.

Odour: Practically odourless.

Activity: Rutin is a member of the group of derivatives of flavone, flavonol and flavonone which enjoy wide distribution in the plant world. These substances occur chiefly as yellow dyestuffs and are of importance for cell metabolism. The effect which these substances exhibit in animal experiments are summarized under the term "Vitamin P activity". Rutin normalises an increased permeability of the capillaries which manifests itself in — among others — intensified lymph circulation, increased protein discharge and a tendency towards oedema. Rutin also normalises reduced capillary resistance characterized by an increased tendency towards capillary bleeding.

The effect of rutin on capillary permeability for colloidal dissolved dyes and on the inhibition of oedema formation, as well as on the suppression of suction bleeding and urtication, has been demonstrated in clinical testing. The effect may possibly be traced back to the ability of rutin to exert an inhibitary effect on the enzyme hyaluronidase, which increases permeability by breaking down hyaluronic acid. Rutin also takes part in calcium metabolism. Quercetin — the aglucone of rutin — is attributed with the character of a redox catalyst.

In man also, results are similar to those obtained in clinical testing in that rutin has a pronounced protective and curative effect on all symptoms accompanying increased capillary fragility and membrane permeability.

The criterion of the effectiveness of rutin therapy used by most workers is the return to normality of a previously abnormal vascular function.